# My World

# Shape

## Ann Peat

**www.raintreepublishers.co.uk**
Visit our website to find out more information about **Raintree** books.

To order:
☎ Phone 44 (0) 1865 888112
📄 Send a fax to 44 (0) 1865 314091
💻 Visit the Heinemann Bookshop at **www.raintreepublishers.co.uk** to browse our catalogue and order online.

First published in Great Britain by Raintree, Halley Court, Jordan Hill, Oxford OX2 8EJ, part of Harcourt Education.
Raintree is a registered trademark of Harcourt Education Ltd.

Editorial: Charlotte Guillain and Diyan Leake
Design: Michelle Lisseter
Picture Research: Maria Joannou
Production: Lorraine Hicks

Originated by Dot Gradations
Printed and bound in China by South China Printing Company

ISBN 1 844 21270 X (hardback)
07 06 05 04 03
10 9 8 7 6 5 4 3 2 1

ISBN 1 844 21275 0 (paperback)
07 06 05 04 03
10 9 8 7 6 5 4 3 2 1

**British Library Cataloguing in Publication Data**
Peat, Ann
Shape
516.1'5
A full catalogue record for this book is available from the British Library.

**Acknowledgements**
The publishers would like to thank the following for permission to reproduce photographs: Collections/Ashley Cooper p. 9; Trevor Clifford p. 11; Tudor Photography pp. 4, 5, 6, 7, 8, 10, 11, 12, 13, 14, 15, 16, 17, 18, 19, 20, 21, 22, 23, 24.

Cover photograph, reproduced with permission of Pete Morris.

Every effort has been made to contact copyright holders of any material reproduced in this book. Any omissions will be rectified in subsequent printings if notice is given to the publishers.

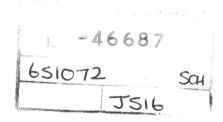

# Contents

Some words are shown in bold, **like this.** You can find them in the glossary on page 24.

# What do flat shapes look like?

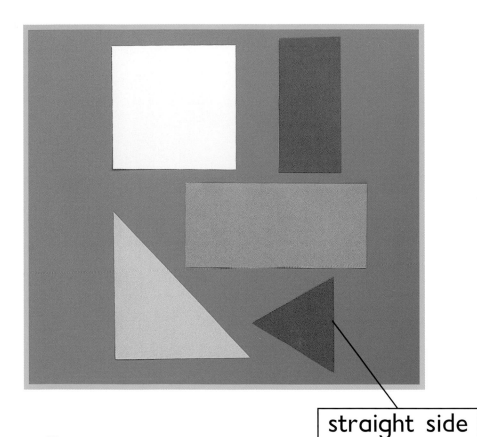

straight side

Some flat shapes have **straight** sides.

curved side

Some flat shapes have **curved** sides.

# What is a circle?

A circle is a flat shape.

It is round.

Count all the circles you can see
on the **climbing frame**.

# What is a triangle?

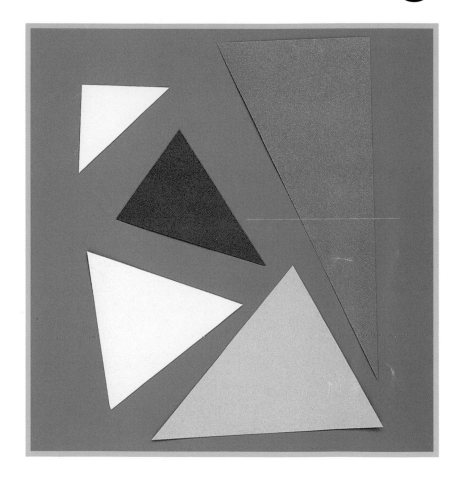

A triangle is a flat shape.

It has three **straight** sides.

How many triangles can you see?

# What is a square?

A square is a flat shape with four sides.

All the sides of a square are the same length.

Where can you see squares in your house?

# What is a rectangle?

A rectangle is a flat shape.

It has two long sides and two shorter sides.

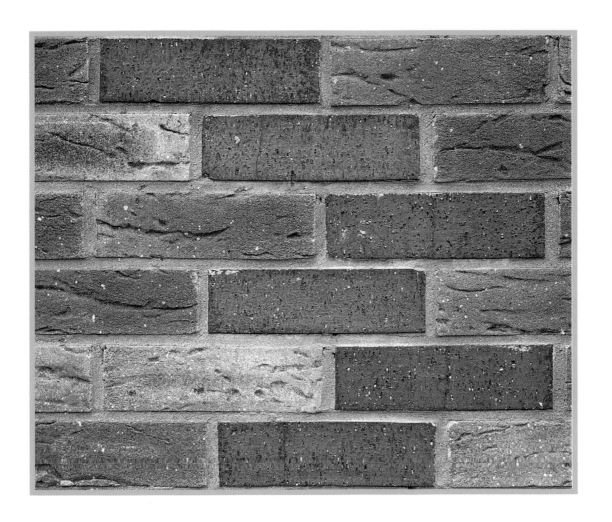

How many blue rectangles can you see in the picture?

# What do solid shapes look like?

straight edge

Solid shapes have edges.

Some edges are **straight**.

curved edge

Some edges are **curved**.

# What else do solid shapes have?

flat face

Solid shapes have faces.

Some faces are flat.

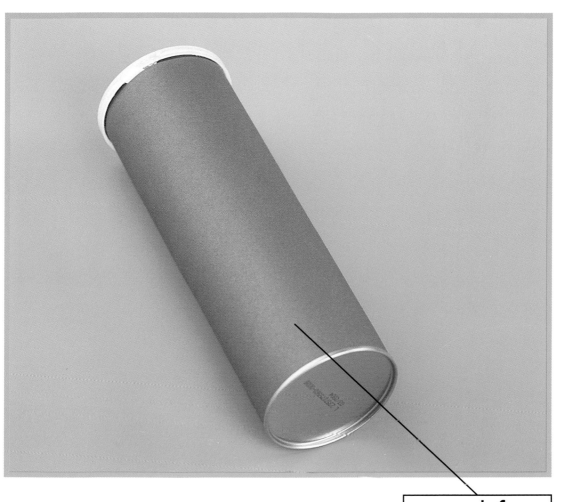

curved face

Some faces are **curved**.

# What solid shapes have flat faces?

cube

cuboid

A cube is a solid shape with six square faces.

A cuboid is a solid shape with six faces.

Some of the faces on a cuboid may be rectangles.

Which of the boxes are cubes and which are cuboids?

# What solid shapes have curved faces?

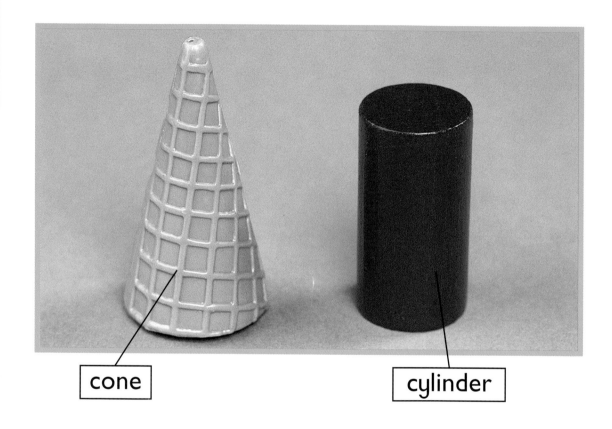

cone

cylinder

A cone is a solid shape with a **curved** face.

One end is pointed.

The other end is a circle.

A cylinder is a solid shape with a curved face.

Each end of a cylinder is a circle.

Try and make a cylinder out of paper.

# What is a sphere?

A sphere is a solid shape that is **curved** all over.

Most balls are spheres.

How many spheres can you see in this picture?

# Glossary

**climbing frame**
framework you can climb on for fun and exercise

**curved**
line or shape with a bend

**straight**
line or shape without a bend

# Index

24